To parents This maze illustrates a walk around town. Children who are trying mazes for the first time can easily draw a line because the path is wide.

■ Draw a line from the arrow (➡) to the star (★) by following the path.

Going Home

■ Draw a line from the arrow (→) to the star (★) by following the path.

A Trip to See Rabbit

Name

Date

To parents It may help your child if he or she traces the path with his or her finger before using a pencil. However, the most important thing is that your child enjoys using a pencil with the maze.

■ Draw a line from the arrow (➜) to the star (★) by following the path.

Visit the Library

■ Draw a line from the arrow (→) to the star (★) by following the path.

A Play Date with Giraffe

Name .... Date ....

To parents   It is okay if your child draws a line off the path. Offer lots of praise when your child arrives at the end of the maze.

■ Draw a line from the arrow (➡) to the star (★) by following the path.

Finding Cat's House

■ Draw a line from the arrow (→) to the star (★) by following the path.

Sending Mail at the Post Office

Name   Date

To parents Encourage your child to hold a pencil correctly. If he or she can not do so, hold the pencil with your child.

■ Draw a line from the arrow (➡) to the star (★) by following the path.

On Our Way to the Park

■ Draw a line from the arrow (→) to the star (★) by following the path.

Skip to the Seafood Store

Name   Date

To parents   When your child is finished, you can talk about the buildings in the town.

■ Draw a line from the arrow (➡) to the star (★) by following the path.

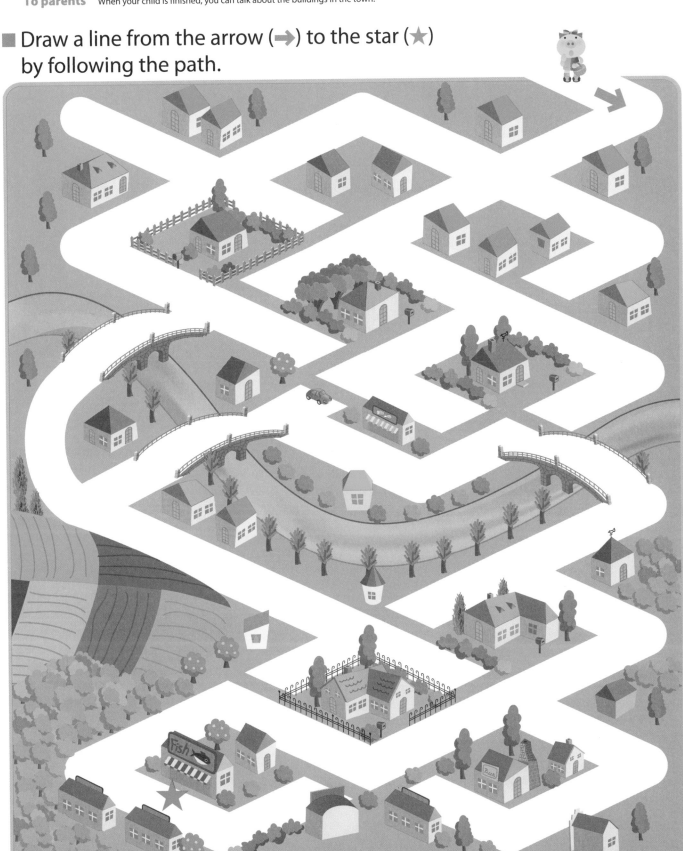

9

Buying Flowers

■ Draw a line from the arrow (→) to the star (★) by following the path.

Let's Go Out to Eat

Name   Date

To parents   Don't forget that the most important thing is that your child enjoys using a pencil with the maze.

■ Draw a line from the arrow (➡) to the star (★) by following the path.

Run to the Bakery

■ Draw a line from the arrow (➡) to the star (★) by following the path.

Soccer

Name

Date

To parents From this page on, the mazes will become more difficult. Encourage your child to first trace the maze with his or her finger before using a pencil.

■ Draw a line from the arrow (➡) to the star (★) by following the path.

Gymnastics

■ Draw a line from the arrow (➡) to the star (★) by following the path.

To parents   It is okay if your child cannot complete the maze neatly. When your child is finished, give him or her a lot of praise.

■ Draw a line from the arrow (➡) to the star (★) by following the path.

Ping Pong

■ Draw a line from the arrow (➡) to the star (★) by following the path.

To parents   If your child is having difficulty holding the pencil, please hold it with your child.

■ Draw a line from the arrow (➡) to the star (★) by following the path.

Ride On

■ Draw a line from the arrow (➡) to the star (★) by following the path.

To parents Don't forget to offer encouragement like, "You can draw a line very well!" Your child will enjoy using a pencil and completing mazes even more if he or she is praised.

■ Draw a line from the arrow (➡) to the star (★) by following the path.

Hopscotch

■ Draw a line from the arrow (➡) to the star (★) by following the path.

Wake Up!

Name.. Date........................

To parents   The path of the maze will gradually become longer. When your child is finished, you can say "You wake up on time, too."

■ Draw a line from the arrow (➡) to the star (★) by following the path.

Toast

■ Draw a line from the arrow (➡) to the star (★) by following the path.

On My Way

Name   Date

To parents When the maze is complex, it is likely your child will go off the path. When your child arrives at the end of the maze without resting, offer lots of praise.

■ Draw a line from the arrow (→) to the star (★) by following the path.

Unicycle

■ Draw a line from the arrow (→) to the star (★) by following the path.

Jumping Rope

Name

Date

To parents When your child is finished, you can talk about jumping rope and other fun activities. You can ask, "Can you jump rope?"

■ Draw a line from the arrow (➡) to the star (★) by following the path.

Baseball

■ Draw a line from the arrow (➡) to the star (★) by following the path.

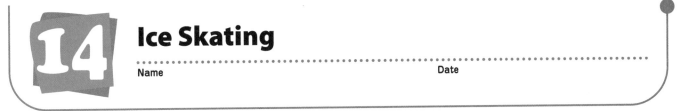

14 Ice Skating

Name

Date

To parents The maze will gradually become more difficult. Before using a pencil, it is okay for your child to confirm the correct direction with his or her finger.

■ Draw a line from the arrow (➡) to the star (★) by following the path.

At the Finish Line!

■ Draw a line from the arrow (➡) to the star (★) by following the path.

Marching Band

Name

Date

To parents This is a complex maze. When your child is finished, offer lots of praise.

■ Draw a line from the arrow (➡) to the star (★) by following the path.

Pilots in Training

■ Draw a line from the arrow (➡) to the star (★) by following the path.

Halloween

Name

Date

To parents If your child seems to be having difficulty, you can help by asking, "Where is the next opening in the maze?"

■ Draw a line from the arrow (➡) to the star (★) by following the path.

Skateboard

■ Draw a line from the arrow (→) to the star (★) by following the path.

17 Thanksgiving

Name

Date

■ Draw a line from the arrow (➡) to the star (★) by following the path.

Ice Hockey

■ Draw a line from the arrow (➡) to the star (★) by following the path.

To parents The mazes are becoming much longer. Encourage your child to complete the maze. When he or she is done, give your child a lot of praise, such as, "Good job on finishing such a long maze!"

■ Draw a line from the arrow () to the star (★) by following the path.

Cycling

■ Draw a line from the arrow (→) to the star (★) by following the path.

Mother's Day

To parents After completing the maze, talk with your child about different holidays and celebrations.

■ Draw a line from the arrow (➡) to the star (★) by following the path.

Hiking

Draw a line from the arrow (➡) to the star (★) by following the path.

20 Show Choir

Name   Date

To parents   How is the line that your child drew? Perhaps it is better than his or her previous work. Please tell your child how he or she is improving and offer lots of praise.

■ Draw a line from the arrow (➡) to the star (★) by following the path.

Football

■ Draw a line from the arrow (➡) to the star (★) by following the path.

21 Concert

Name

Date

To parents The mazes will gradually become longer. When your child arrives at the goal without resting, offer lots of praise.

■ Draw a line from the arrow (➡) to the star (★) by following the path.

Spin on the Teacup Ride

■ Draw a line from the arrow (➡) to the star (★) by following the path.

Playing Dress-up

Name

Date

To parents This maze has many turns. Your child will need to use a pencil carefully, so watch him or her closely.

■ Draw a line from the arrow (➡) to the star (★) by following the path.

Basketball

■ Draw a line from the arrow (➡) to the star (★) by following the path.

To parents It is good to talk with your child about each illustration. You can ask something like, "What is your favorite holiday?"

■ Draw a line from the arrow (➡) to the star (★) by following the path.

Gifts

■ Draw a line from the arrow (➡) to the star (★) by following the path.

Bus Trip

To parents   This maze is more complex than the previous maze. When your child completes this exercise, you can say, "You are great at mazes!"

■ Draw a line from the arrow (➡) to the star (★) by following the path.

Submarine

■ Draw a line from the arrow (➡) to the star (★) by following the path.

Fire Engine

Name　　　　　　　　　　　　　　　　　　　　Date

To parents When your child is finished, you can talk about fire emergencies. You can start by saying, "When do people call a fire engine?"

■ Draw a line from the arrow (➡) to the star (★) by following the path.

Choo Choo!

■ Draw a line from the arrow (➡) to the star (★) by following the path.

■ Draw a line from the arrow (➡) to the star (★) by following the path.

Twisting Maze

■ Draw a line from the arrow (→) to the star (★) by following the path.

Zigzag Maze

Name

Date

To parents This maze is made by combining straight lines in different orientations. Your child may take some time to find the correct path. When your child is finished, offer lots of praise.

■ Draw a line from the arrow (➡) to the star (★) by following the path.

53

Winding Maze

■ Draw a line from the arrow (➡) to the star (★) by following the path.

54

28

Spinning Maze

Name   Date

To parents   This maze is made by combining curved lines. Your child may go at a slower pace because he or she must follow the circular shapes. Encourage your child to draw the path slowly and steadily.

■ Draw a line from the arrow (→) to the star (★) by following the path.

Slanting Maze

■ Draw a line from the arrow (➡) to the star (★) by following the path.

Swivel Maze

Name   Date

To parents   This maze is made by combining straight and curved lines. Encourage your child to draw the path slowly and steadily.

■ Draw a line from the arrow (➡) to the star (★) by following the path.

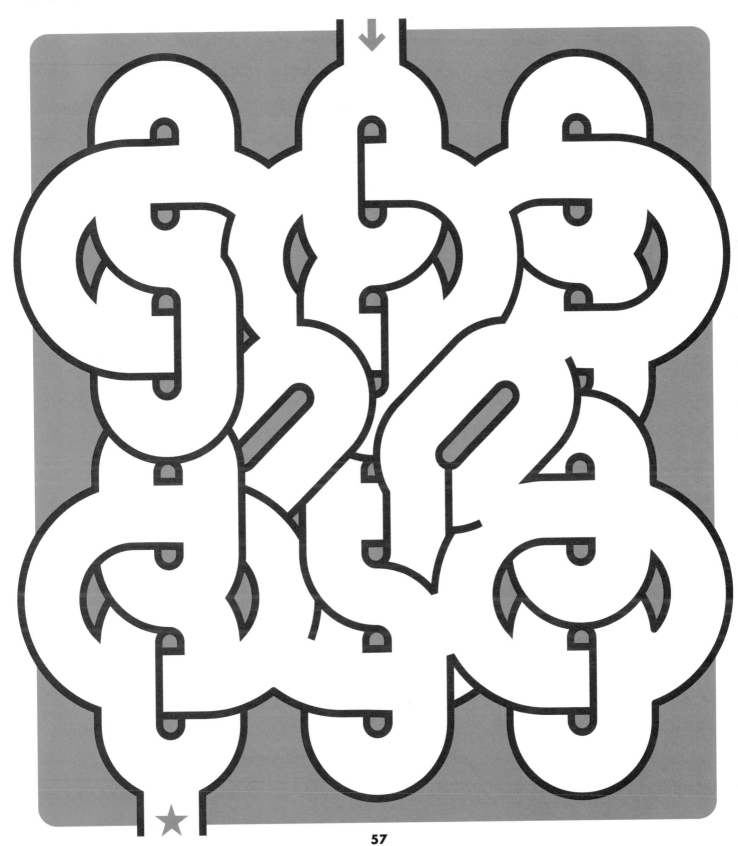

Turning Maze

Draw a line from the arrow (➡) to the star (★) by following the path.

Whirling maze

Name   Date

To parents   This maze is more complex. It is okay if your child cannot arrive at the goal without making a few mistakes. When your child is finished, offer lots of praise.

■ Draw a line from the arrow (➡) to the star (★) by following the path.

Twirling Maze

■ Draw a line from the arrow (➡) to the star (★) by following the path.

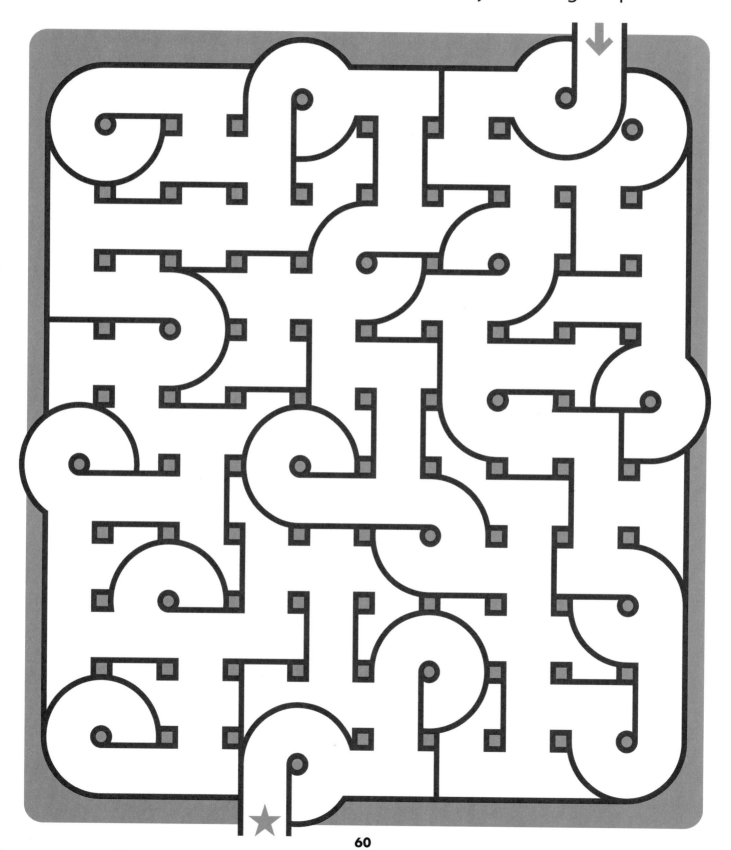

31 Crazy Maze

Name   Date

To parents   This is the last section of the book. When your child has finished the book, compare this page with his or her previous work. You will see a lot of progress in your child's ability to use a pencil smoothly.

■ Draw a line from the arrow (➡) to the star (★) by following the path.

Mixed Maze

■ Draw a line from the arrow (➡) to the star (★) by following the path.

KUM◯N

Certificate of Achievement

is hereby congratulated on completing

Are You Ready for Kindergarten? Pencil Skills

Presented on

, 20

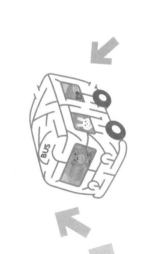

Parent or Guardian